LET'S TALK ABOUT... KINKS AND FETISHES

Questions and Conversation Starters for Couples Exploring Their Kinky Wild Side

What turns *you* on?

J.R. James

Beyond the Sheets Series

Book 3

All rights reserved. No portion of this book may be reproduced in any form without permission from the publisher, except as permitted by U.S. copyright law.

This book is for entertainment purposes only. This book is not intended, nor should the reader consider it, to be relational advice for any situation. The author makes no representations or warranties with respect to accuracy, fitness, completeness, or applicability of the contents of this book.

Copyright © 2019 Love & Desire Press

Written by J.R. James

All rights reserved.

ISBN: 978-1-952328-18-3

Spice up your love life even more, and explore all the discussion books for couples by J.R. James:

Love and Relationship Books for Couples

Would You Rather...? The Romantic Conversation Game for Couples (Love and Romance Edition)

Sexy Game Books for Couples

Would You Rather...? The Naughty Conversation Game for Couples (Hot and Sexy Edition)

Truth or Dare? The Sexy Game of Naughty Choices (Hot and Wild Edition)

Never Have I Ever... An Exciting and Sexy Game for Adults (Hot and Dirty Edition)

The Hot or Not Quiz for Couples: The Sexy Game of Naughty Questions and Revealing Answers

Pillow Talk: The Sexy Game of Naughty Trivia Questions for Couples

The Naughty Newlywed Game: A Sexy Game of Questions for Couples

Sexy Discussion Books for Couples

Let's Talk Sexy: Essential Conversation Starters to Explore Your Lover's Secret Desires and Transform Your Sex Life

All **THREE** *Let's Talk About...* sexy question books in one massive volume for one low price. Save now!

Let's Talk About... Sexual Fantasies and Desires: Questions and Conversation Starters for Couples Exploring Their Sexual Interests

Let's Talk About... Non-Monogamy: Questions and Conversation Starters for Couples Exploring Open Relationships, Swinging, or Polyamory

Let's Talk About... Kinks and Fetishes: Questions and Conversation Starters for Couples Exploring Their Sexual Wild Side

Change your sex life forever through the power of sexy fun with your spouse, partner, or lover!

www.sexygamesforcouples.com

Sexy Vacations for Couples
https://geni.us/Passion

What This Book is About

Sometimes, even the most loving couples can fall into predictable, boring, or stale sexual patterns. When they find themselves in a sexual rut, the erotic excitement that once excited them can feel like a distant memory. Breaking free of routine is one of the many reasons a couple might explore the world of kink. Some people already know, deep down inside, they have this "one little thing" that really, *really* turns them on. Maybe it's spanking, or voyeurism, or domination— or something else, but whatever it may be, they get a special thrill whenever they have the chance to live out that fantasy. Now's your opportunity to discover and discuss your kink!

Through a variety of questions which you and your partner take turns asking one another, this book will guide you through discussions about kinky possibilities and what *really* turns you both on. It gives you a starting point for the exploration of various kinks and fetishes that might interest you. If your closet is full of cat-o'-nine-tails and latex rubber suits, this book might be too basic for you. But if you're unsure of what you want, yet you know you've got to do *something* to electrify your sex life, then this book can help. So, if you're familiar with shibari or kinbaku, or if you hide a Violet Wand in your dresser drawer, then you might be a bit more advanced that what we're offering here. (We always welcome the kink veterans' feedback though!) If you're ready to discover and name your secret kinks, then let's proceed. After all, even the most seasoned kinksters had to start somewhere, now here's your chance!

First we need to discuss some terminology and clarify a few of the finer points. (For the Kink connoisseurs, please understand I'm really generalizing for simplicity's sake here.) For those of you who don't know it already: kinks are basically anything outside of the box of "normal" sexual behavior, and fetishes demand some sort of object for sexual gratification. As an example, swinging could be considered a "kink", while a sexual attraction to feet could be considered a "fetish". All fetishes are kinks, but not all kinks are fetishes. As you can imagine, since there are SO many things outside of "normal" sexual behavior, there's also an endless variety of kinks and fetishes. These questions will deal with the more common and popular ones.

The three most important things to remember when we're speaking about kinky sex are: **CONSENT**, **CONSENT**, and **CONSENT**. If you're going to play in the world of kink, you need to be absolutely certain that everyone involved is on the same page at all times. Remember, what gives kinky pleasure to one person, can be uncomfortable or even disgusting for another. That's why discussion is critical for both pleasure and safety's sake. Some kinks can be either physically or emotionally dangerous, and you must make certain that all parties involved have given their explicit and clear consent every time.

It's also helpful to know that many, many kinks may intersect with one another or overlap. For instance, while bondage is technically BDSM, it may also involve a little domination. In the right circumstances, swinging could also be considered group sex. Again, for simplicity's sake, we're not saying that every kink we've included in the book falls "hard and fast" into one category, it could easily fall in multiple categories. We just wanted to give you some idea of the categories involved.

Now that we've covered those points, let's move on to the questions themselves. This book is set up slightly different than our other *Beyond the Sheets* books. We still have the discussion questions on each page, but listed beneath each question is the kink or fetish that may interest you depending on your answers. Remember, this is just to help you name that kink so you can pursue more information about it if you wish. Ready to explore? Then, let's go!

What This Book is Not

This book may push your boundaries. That being said, it is not intended for insecure couples or individuals, or those who might be prone to jealousy.

This book is not intended to replace therapeutic discussion and is for entertainment purposes only. If you and a partner have sexual or relational problems, we strongly recommend seeing a sex or marriage therapist.

We are not recommending any of the things in this book, nor do we encourage any actions or behaviors outside of a person's comfort limits. In addition, we do not encourage or recommend any unsafe sex practices.

The conversation starters in this book are not meant to be a comprehensive list of every kink or fetish. We have specifically excluded kinks that could be considered "extreme", whether physically or emotionally. We have also excluded kinks that could be triggering for those with sexual trauma in their past. These questions are simply starters that may lead you into deeper discussions or exploration. So please, feel free to elaborate and improvise on the questions. ;)

1

If your lover had a wand that when touched to your skin felt like the tickle of warm champagne, would you be sexually aroused?

(Electrical play)

2

During sex do you like your lover to kiss, lick, or blow on your nipples?

(Nipple play)

3

Have you ever fantasized about being a stripper or wondered what it'd be like giving lap dances to strangers?

(Exhibitionism)

4

Have you ever been curious about "sex clubs"? Are you willing to visit one just to see what it's like?

(Swinging)

5

Do you ever want to be "used" as a play thing? Would you like to be a "living sex toy"?

(Submission)

6

Is the thought of feeding your partner while they're blindfolded erotic?

(Food play)

7

After having sex with your lover, do you ever feel like you could just keep going and going? Is it hard to satisfy your sexual appetite?

(Gangbangs)

8

Would you like your lover to submit to your every whim? Would you like them to be your "love slave" and fulfill your sexual requests?

(Domination)

9

Your partner is being fucked by another sexy person and all you can do is watch it happen. You hear their moans of pleasure while they're writhing together on the bed, and you're just sitting there. Are you turned on?

(Cuckolding or Cuckqueaning)

10

Do you enjoy it when your partner slips their finger in your rectum while the two of you are having sex?

(Anal play or pegging)

11

How would you like to be held in your partner's arms as they coo and coddle you, rocking you back and forth?

(Adult babies)

12

How would it feel to have your entire body wrapped in tight latex rubber? With every move you make, you feel it stretching against your skin. If you like the idea, describe what you would do while wearing it.

(Latex rubber fetish)

13

Do you ever desire your lover to take control during sex? Would you like them to be more in charge of the sexual situation?

(Submission)

14

What costume or uniform would you like me to wear before sex? What would you like to wear?

(Role playing)

15

Do you think pain can ever be pleasurable? If so, describe a scene you would find sexually arousing.

(BDSM)

16

Are your partner's feet especially attractive? Is there something about them that you're drawn towards?

(Foot fetish)

17

Do you enjoy getting your ass slapped during sex? Do you want harder and more frequent slapping?

(Spanking)

18

Have you ever fantasized about being the opposite gender, or wearing that gender's clothing?

(Cross-dressing)

19

Is the idea of having your arms held down while your lover powerfully ravages you exciting? If so, describe a scene that would make you hot.

(Submission)

20

Imagine you're on an overnight camping trip with friends. Somehow, it has turned into a group make out session around the fire. Someone suggests they all go into a tent together. Do you say "yes"? If so, what happens in the tent?

(Group sex)

21

If while taking a shower with your lover, they knelt in front of you and asked you to pee on them, would you? How would you feel about it?

(Watersports)

22

How does the sensation of tight leather wrapped around your skin make you feel? Are leather pants or jackets sexy in nature?

(Leather play)

23

Would you like your partner to handcuff you to the bed while they slowly explore your body with their tongue?

(Bondage)

24

Are you interested in a threesome? A foursome? A "moresome"? Describe what you'd like to experience.

(Swinging)

25

Imagine entering a small store, but you don't see any shoppers or sales people. As you make your way to the back of the store, you hear moans of pleasure coming from a dressing room and it's obvious the two people in there are fucking. Are you turned on knowing you can hear them, but they don't know you're there?

(Voyeurism)

26

Do you want your lover to anally stimulate you? How do you feel about them using a vibrator anally on you?

(Anal play or pegging)

27
How would you feel about having sex in a public place where people might be able to see you?

(Exhibitionism)

28

Would you like to have a lover straddle you and drip wax from a candle onto your bare chest?

(Wax play)

29

Is static electricity an erotic sensation?

(Electrical play)

30

Is it hot to think about your partner going on a date without you, having hot and wild sex, and then coming home to tell you all about it?

(Cuckolding or Cuckqueaning)

31

Is it exciting to think about your lover making you cry out in shock or surprise by an unexpected slap during sex?

(BDSM)

32

Would you like to cover your lover in chocolate sauce and lick it off them? If not chocolate, would you like to use a different food?

(Food play)

33

Have you ever fantasized about being forced to watch your partner pleasure someone else?

(Cuckolding or Cuckqueaning)

34

Would you like to act out a sexual scene with your partner? What would it look like? What do you want your partner to do or say?

(Role playing)

35

Is the thought of pinning down your lover and holding their wrists while you fuck them exciting? Do you want to be on top and in charge?

(Domination)

36

How would you like to be bent over your partner's knee and spanked? Is it a turn on?

(Spanking)

37

Are you turned on by the idea of squirting? If you're female, have you ever squirted when orgasming?

(Watersports)

38

You're at a party and having a great time. It seems a group of friends have moved into a bedroom and are taking off their clothes. It's obvious they're all about to have sex. Are you interested in joining them?

(Group sex)

39

Do you like it when your lover bites or pinches your nipples? If so, do you prefer it rough or gentle?

(Nipple play)

40

Does the idea of cuddling with your lover while wearing adult diapers and being treated like a baby fascinate you?

(Adult babies)

41

Imagine you walk in late to a movie theater and sit in the back row. There's only one other couple in the theater, and they're sitting in the front row. They don't even realize you're there. Before you know it, they're fucking each other loudly. What do you do?

(Voyeurism)

42

Does the idea of being treated like a pet or an animal by your lover turn you on?

(Pet play)

43

Is the idea of multiple people sexually pleasing you at the same time sound hot? Imagine one person after another consecutively fucking you until you're exhausted. Does that turn you on?

(Gangbangs)

44

Are you turned on by the idea of using a cucumber or other vegetable as a dildo?

(Food play)

45

Are you interested in wearing leather corsets or shorts?

(Leather play)

46

Have you ever wanted to suck on a lover's toes?

(Foot fetish)

47

Would having your feet and hands bound with rope feel exciting?

(Bondage)

48

You, your partner, and your best friend are hanging out for the evening. On a silly dare, your partner and your friend start making out? What would you like to happen next?

(Swinging)

49

Do you enjoy anal sex? Is it the giving or the receiving that you normally enjoy? Would you be willing to switch it up?

(Anal play or pegging)

50

Do you feel sex is a spiritual experience? Would you like to learn how to prolong the experience and share erotic energy with your partner in more than just a physical sense?

(Tantra)

51

Would you enjoy commanding your lover not to move while you sexually tease them? Is it a turn on to watch them try and obey?

(Domination)

52

If your lover was straddling you naked and the two of you were making out, how would you feel if suddenly they peed all over your lap? Turned on, or turned off?

(Watersports)

53

Does the thought of a lover gently whipping your body with leather straps make you hot and excited?

(BDSM)

54

Do you ever imagine sexy scenarios with your partner in which you both are playing a role? For instance, a "student" has to stay after class with the "teacher"?

(Role playing)

55

If you and your lover were on a beach, lying in the sun and making out, would you get turned on knowing other people were watching the two of you?

(Exhibitionism)

56

Is it erotic to think about your partner comparing you to another lover? What if they were telling you how much better the other person was in bed?

(Cuckolding or Cuckqueaning)

57

How would you like to be blindfolded and commanded by your partner to obey their requests? Would you enjoy being obedient?

(Submission)

58

Is there something sensual or arousing about the thought of struggling while being restrained?

(Bondage)

59

Would you like to be the disciplinarian in a sexual relationship?

(Domination)

60

Does the idea of your lover saying filthy things and swearing during sex turn you on? What would you like to hear them say?

(Dirty talk)

61

Would you like to masturbate in front of your lover (or other people)?

(Exhibitionism)

62

Would you like your partner to use their feet or toes to get you off?

(Foot fetish)

63

Can jealousy or humiliation ever feel sexually arousing?

(Cuckolding or Cuckqueaning)

64

Is wearing a shiny and tight body suit a sexy idea?

(Latex rubber fetish)

65

How would you feel if your partner put a collar and leash on you? What if they made you eat out of a bowl on the ground?

(Pet play)

66

How would you like to feel your lover slide their tongue between your buttocks and lick your anus? Would you like to try it on them too?

(Rimming)

67

Imagine your lover softly caressing a feather all over your naked body while you lie on your back? Would the tickling sensation be a sexual charge?

(Tickling fetish)

68

Do you like rough sex? Is the thought of getting bit and your hair pulled sexually exciting?

(BDSM)

69

Would you like to be woken up to your partner fondling you or giving you oral sex? Does the sight of your sleeping lover sexually excite you?

(Sleep sex)

70

Is it erotic to have sex with your lover while they're fully dressed? How about if you have on all your clothing too?

(Fully clothed fetish)

71

Would it turn you on to watch a couple have sex on security camera footage?

(Voyeurism)

72

Is the idea of a hot, sweaty tangle of people having group sex something that entices you? Have you ever wanted to experience an orgy?

(Group sex)

73

What would you think if you and your partner went on a double date with another couple and everyone ended up in bed together? If you like the idea, is there a couple you could imagine joining you in the bedroom?

(Swinging)

74

Would you like to visit a nude beach or resort?

(Exhibitionism)

75

Is there something primal, erotic, and sexy about fire? Is feeling the warmth of an open flame sensual?

(Fire play)

76

Do you enjoy having your chest massaged or your nipples sucked?

(Nipple play)

77

Is the sensation of wearing spandex or tight, slick clothing a turn-on? Do you enjoy seeing your lover wear items like that?

(Latex rubber fetish)

78

Is it exciting to think about being thrown to the wall and spanked hard?

(BDSM)

79

Do you ever want to see your lover dress the opposite of how they normally would? For instance, a feminine lady dressed in construction worker clothes, or a masculine guy dressed in lingerie?

(Cross-dressing)

80

Do you ever like to pretend your lover is somebody else during sex?

(Role playing)

81

Could referring to your partner as "Sir", "Madam", "Master", or "Mistress" during sex be a turn on to you? Does being "beneath" them feel erotic?

(Submission)

82

Imagine lying naked in bed while lightly restrained and blindfolded. Your partner teases you in a variety of ways and never says a word. Does it sound sexually exciting?

(Sensation play)

83
Would you like to be gagged by your lover while they ravish you?

(BDSM)

84

Would you enjoy being disciplined by your lover with a paddle?

(Spanking)

85

Does being fucked from behind with a dildo or a penis sound good to you? Does it excite you?

(Anal play or pegging)

86

Have you ever wanted to lick whipped cream off your lover's body?

(Food play)

87

Imagine having to remain completely silent during sex, no words or sounds. Does it sound like an erotic challenge?

(Silent play)

88

If you and your lover pretended you were complete strangers that met, and then had hot passionate sex, would you enjoy the experience, or find it strange?

(Role playing)

89

Have you ever become sexually aroused in the middle of a "tickle fight"?

(Tickling fetish)

90

Do stockings or socks on attractive feet turn you on? How about a sexy person taking off their shoes?

(Foot fetish)

91

If your partner had the ability to give you an electric shock anywhere on your body at will, would you be interested?

(Electrical play)

92

Are you interested in feeling a deeper, more sensual sexual experience with your lover?

(Tantra)

93

Would you be willing to have your hands tied together and hung from the ceiling, your lover teasing your body as you stand there helpless?

(Bondage)

94

How would you like the sensation of a thin rod smacking the bottom of your bare feet?

(Caning)

95

Have you ever enjoyed sex with your lover while both of you are wearing your underwear or panties pushed to the side?

(Fully clothed fetish)

96

Does the thought of making love to your partner in front of a room full of strangers turn you on? If so, describe the most erotic thing about it?

(Exhibitionism)

97

Is it thrilling to imagine having no way of seeing or hearing what your lover may do to you in bed? Every sensation would be a surprise.

(Sensation play)

98

Is the act of urinating ever sexually arousing to you?

(Watersports)

99

Do you ever fantasize about being the complete center of sexual attention in a group of people? All of them are only there to please you. Interested?

(Gangbangs)

100

Do you have your nipples pierced, or are you interested in getting them pierced?

(Nipple play)

101

Is it sexually thrilling to imagine getting "punished" in the bedroom by your lover?

(BDSM)

102

Have you ever wanted your partner to slide an ice cube over your naked body?

(Sensation play)

103
Would you be interested in having your partner tell you exactly what to wear in a sexual scenario?

(Submission)

104

Would you like to see someone bigger, stronger, or more attractive than yourself sexually gratify your partner?

(Cuckolding or Cuckqueaning)

105

Is it a turn on to think of your lover groveling as they kneel in front of you? How about if you made them kiss your feet?

(Domination)

106
Are there any kinks or fetishes not in this book that interest you?

107
Would you like to try any of these kinks we've discussed tonight?

Spice up your love life even more, and explore all the discussion books for couples by J.R. James:

Love and Relationship Books for Couples

Would You Rather...? The Romantic Conversation Game for Couples (Love and Romance Edition)

Sexy Game Books for Couples

Would You Rather...? The Naughty Conversation Game for Couples (Hot and Sexy Edition)

Truth or Dare? The Sexy Game of Naughty Choices (Hot and Wild Edition)

Never Have I Ever... An Exciting and Sexy Game for Adults (Hot and Dirty Edition)

The Hot or Not Quiz for Couples: The Sexy Game of Naughty Questions and Revealing Answers

Pillow Talk: The Sexy Game of Naughty Trivia Questions for Couples

The Naughty Newlywed Game: A Sexy Game of Questions for Couples

Sexy Discussion Books for Couples

Let's Talk Sexy: Essential Conversation Starters to Explore Your Lover's Secret Desires and Transform Your Sex Life

All **THREE** *Let's Talk About...* sexy question books in one massive volume for one low price. Save now!

Let's Talk About... Sexual Fantasies and Desires: Questions and Conversation Starters for Couples Exploring Their Sexual Interests

Let's Talk About... Non-Monogamy: Questions and Conversation Starters for Couples Exploring Open Relationships, Swinging, or Polyamory

Let's Talk About... Kinks and Fetishes: Questions and Conversation Starters for Couples Exploring Their Sexual Wild Side

Change your sex life forever through the power of sexy fun with your spouse, partner, or lover!

www. sexygamesforcouples.com

Sexy Vacations for Couples
https://geni.us/Passion

ABOUT THE AUTHOR

J.R. James is a best-selling author who has a passion for bringing couples closer together and recharging their sexual intimacy. Erotic discussion is a powerfully sexy thing, and his conversation starter books have helped many couples reach new and sexually exciting heights in their relationships!

Sexy conversation with your partner is a magical, bonding experience. Through these best-selling question books, couples can find an easy way to engage in open and honest sexual discussion with each other. The result is a relationship that is both erotically charged and sexually liberating.

www.ingramcontent.com/pod-product-compliance
Lightning Source LLC
Chambersburg PA
CBHW071719020426
42333CB00017B/2334